A souvenir guide

Scotney Castle

Kent

A Work of Art and N 2

Tour of the House 10

Tour of the Garden 28

The Estate 34

 National Trust

A Work of Art and Nature

Scotney is not one, but two houses, united by art and nature. Surrounded by the moat at the bottom of the valley are the romantic ruins of the medieval castle. At the top of the hill is the new house, built in 1837–43 for Edward Hussey III. The carefully contrived views between new and old represent almost the last, and perhaps the most perfect, expression of the Picturesque landscape style.

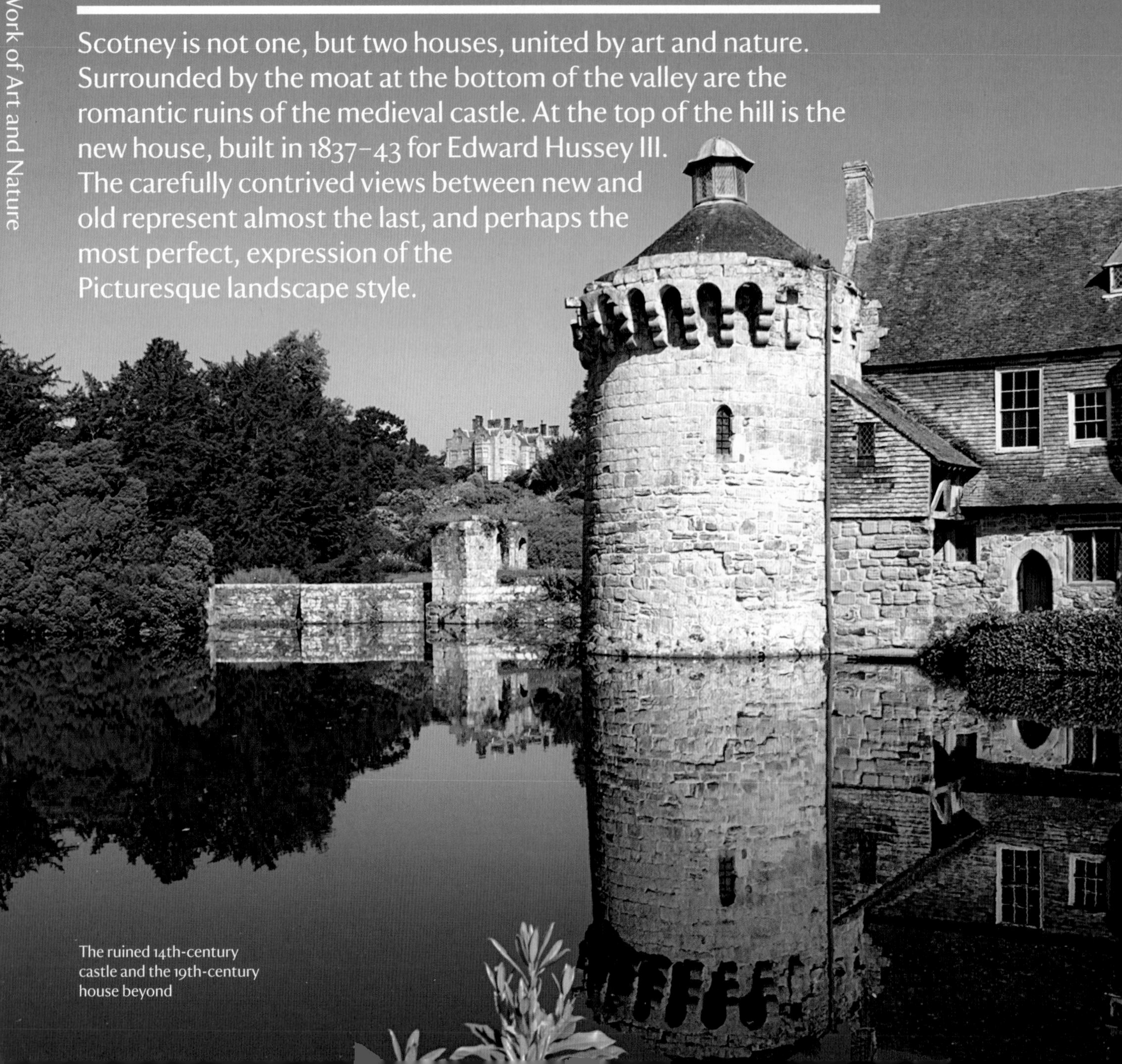

The ruined 14th-century castle and the 19th-century house beyond

Above The Husseys at home. From left to right: Major William Hussey, Brig.-Gen. Arthur Hussey, Mildred Hussey, Henrietta Hussey, Edward Hussey III, Sir Ralph Anstruther, Gertrude Hussey, Henry Hussey, Edward Windsor Hussey

Edward Hussey III spent many happy years at Scotney with his wife and children, but only two more generations of the family have lived here since then. Perhaps partly for that reason, the new house has been little altered. But Scotney has always been a welcoming and sociable place, filled with books and paintings, many of which were created by the Husseys.

Faithful to the Hussey family motto (‘*Vix ea nostra voco*’: ‘I scarcely call these things our own’), in 1970 Edward's grandson, Christopher Hussey, gave Scotney to the National Trust. The garden has been open for many years. Following the death of Christopher's widow Betty, you can see inside the new house.

The garden today

Within the Picturesque composition devised by Edward Hussey III, the planting has been enriched over almost two centuries to emphasise bold shape and strong colour throughout the year. The Great Storm of 1987 shattered the picture, but the fallen cedars and cypresses have been replaced, and the new exposed areas offered opportunities for experiment. While man-made gardens are always in a state of flux, the wild flowers, which are such an important part of the wider Scotney landscape, maintain their natural cycle.

The Picturesque garden

From the early 18th century, British landscape gardeners had been creating gardens inspired by pictures, but by 1800 a reaction had set in. Critics like the Rev. William Gilpin considered the grassy vistas designed by ‘Capability’ Brown too smooth and tidy. They might be beautiful, but they were not *picturesque*: to resemble the best landscape painting, a garden needed drama, variety and rough edges. At Scotney, the plunging site, the mixture of sheltered quarry and open lawn, and the ragged silhouette of the Old Castle provided all three in abundance.

Early history

The secluded Scotney estate lies in the valley of the River Bewl on the Kent/Sussex border and has been inhabited since at least the 12th century. Roger Ashburnham built the castle about 1378–80, apparently in response to the threat of French invasion, although it was always more fortified manor house than fortress. Like nearby Bodiam Castle, it had circular towers at each corner, only one of which, the Ashburnham Tower, still stands; the foundations of the other three form the angles of the east island.

The Darells

For 350 years Scotney Castle was the home of the Catholic Darell family, who rebuilt the south wing adjoining the Ashburnham Tower about 1580. In 1598 they hid the Jesuit Father Richard Blount in the priest's hole which can still be seen in the Old Castle. In the 1630s William Darell demolished much of the castle and used the masonry in a new three-storey east range, of which only the walls (bearing the lion crest of the Darells) are left. Around 1720 George Darell made further alterations, capping the Ashburnham Tower with a cupola and a conical tiled roof. In the mid-18th century family squabbles led to lawsuits, which drained the Darells' resources and forced them to sell Scotney.

The Husseys

In 1778 Edward Hussey bought the castle, and between 1783 and 1792 pieced the rest of the old Darell estate back together. Edward Hussey I (1749–1816) trained as a barrister, but was more interested in cricket than the law, playing frequently for the MCC from its foundation in 1787. Tragically, he committed suicide in the Old Castle. His son, another Edward, survived him by only a year, leaving a widow, Anne. These successive deaths may have prompted Anne to move the family to St Leonards. Here she brought up her son, Edward III (1809–94), who was fascinated from childhood by architecture and landscape gardening. In 1835 he decided to move back to Scotney and build a new house there.

Left The Old Castle from the east, showing a 17th-century range now largely gone

Opposite The circular late 14th-century Ashburnham Tower

Below *Scotney in 1783*; sketch by S.H. Grimm

‘Bless’d too is he, who, ‘midst his tufted trees,
Some ruin’d castle’s lofty towers sees;
Imbosom’d high upon the mountain’s brow,
Or nodding o’er the stream that glides below.’
Richard Payne Knight (1794)

Building the New House

Edward Hussey chose the young architect Anthony Salvin to build his new house. Salvin had already made a reputation designing country houses in an Elizabethan Revival style.

Practicality makes perfect

Hussey had firm views about what he wanted, and it took 33 meetings with his architect before he got it. A practical layout was his first priority: the entrance hall and staircase were placed in the centre of the house, and the main rooms were arranged along the south and east fronts to enjoy the best views of the garden. This arrangement has stood the test of time very well.

Construction began in February 1837, using a streaky golden sandstone dug from the quarry immediately below the house. It was completed in 1843.

The entrance front

The battlemented tower dominates the front elevation, which recalls the medieval pele-towers of Salvin's native Northumbria.

Opposite The garden front

Opposite below The quarry below the New House, c.1845; watercolour by Edward Hussey III

Below The entrance front

Tall chimneys and zig-zagging gables enliven the roofline, while the projecting kitchen quarters on the left and porch and hall bay window on the right give variety to the façade.

Look out for the handsome lead rainwater hoppers, which were designed by the Regency heraldic artist Thomas Willement.

The garden front

Raised up on a grassy mound, this is plainer than the entrance front, because it was designed to look out from, rather than at. The principal feature is the great central window that rises above the Garden Lobby to light the main stairs.

The English style

In the 1830s many people looked back fondly to the reign of Elizabeth I as the era of 'Merry England'. Salvin helped to revive the architectural style of that period, which was seen as supremely English and the perfect choice for the new Houses of Parliament.

Creating the garden

For advice on planting, Hussey turned to the Rev. Gilpin's nephew, William Sawrey Gilpin, who designed the area around the Bastion and devised the spectacular views down to the moat and the Old Castle, which was retained as a pleasantly jumbled ruin of different periods. Wooded parkland on the gently rising slope opposite provided a suitably arcadian backdrop.

Living at Scotney

Left Edward Hussey III, builder of Scotney, with his eldest son Edward, around 1857

Edward Hussey III (1807–94)
Builder of the New House

After all the effort he had taken designing his new house, Edward Hussey was content to enjoy it unaltered for the rest of his long life. He travelled, painted and fulfilled his responsibilities as the local squire. His eldest son, Edward Windsor Hussey (1855–1952), was similarly long-lived and conservative, maintaining the way of life of his Victorian childhood into the 1950s. Prayers were said promptly at nine each morning in the presence of the whole household. Even when there were no guests for supper, he sat at one end of the long table, his wife at the other. The quiet was disturbed only during the Second World War, when the Husseys gave refuge to pupils from the King's School, Rochester.

Christopher Hussey (1899–1970)
Writer and campaigner

The nephew of Edward Windsor Hussey, Christopher Hussey, published his first article for *Country Life* in 1917, while he was still at school. He joined the staff in 1920 and served as editor in 1933–40, continuing to write regularly for it on country houses until his death. Hussey was one of the first to recognise that the historic country houses of Britain were threatened by social and financial changes and to argue that they were worth preserving as a unique aspect of national life. He was an important influence on Lord Lothian, the mastermind of the National

Far left and left Christopher and Betty Hussey painted by their friend John Ward in 1964 and 1965

Trust's Country Houses Scheme, which has done so much to save and open Britain's great houses. He also wrote the classic biography of the architect Edwin Lutyens, whose work he had championed in *Country Life*.

Christopher inherited Scotney from his uncle in 1952. As he himself recalled, 'Care was taken to preserve without falsifying the intrinsic period character of the house'. He spent the last years of his life ensuring that the famous garden was left in good heart for future generations, when he was not campaigning, writing humorous verse, painting or choosing stock for his prize herd of Sussex cattle.

Betty Hussey (1907–2006)
Gardens enthusiast

Christopher Hussey proposed to Elizabeth Kerr-Smiley in the garden at Scotney. Their engagement photograph duly appeared in *Country Life*, and they were married in 1936. When they moved into Scotney, she modernised the antiquated services and introduced her own family furniture and such appropriate period touches as the 1830s curtains bought from the great sale of the contents of Ashburnham Place in Sussex in 1953.

The Husseys spent many happy years at Scotney, entertaining their broad spectrum of friends, who included Margaret and Denis Thatcher, who for a time lived in the Belfry Flat at Scotney.

Below A page from the Husseys' country house album

Tour of the House

The Hall
The Study

The Hall

This room is the heart of the house, connecting conveniently with all the other principal rooms. It is quite simply decorated: plain oak panelling with painted walls.

The entrance porch is balanced by a bay window, which was designed to accommodate that essential of the Victorian country house – a billiard-table. Also typically Victorian is the stone fireplace with its loyal motto 'fear god hono[u]r the king'. The huge 17th-century wrought-iron firedogs were made by local Sussex smiths for the Old Castle. From the start, the fireplaces were supplemented with central heating, from radiators and hot-air vents. The parquet flooring came ready-assembled from Frankfurt.

Furniture

The court cupboard by the front door incorporates panels of 17th-century Flemish woodwork. It was bought by Edward Hussey and is one of the few pieces of antique furniture in the house.

The huge folding screen is covered with rare maps and is placed by the front door to reduce draughts. Much of the other furniture was inherited by Betty Hussey from her parents.

Pictures and sculpture

Christopher and Betty Hussey rehung the 18th-century family portraits in matching black and gilt frames above the panelling. (Previously, there had also been Victorian hunting trophies here.) The Old Masters

Above Christopher Hussey, Man of Letters; medallion by R. Tait McKenzie, 1930

Left The Hall

came mostly from Betty Hussey's family. The views of the New House and the Old Castle over the fireplace and in the bay window were painted by John Piper, who became a friend of the Husseys in the 1940s.

The large medallion of Christopher Hussey on the pier left of the stairs was made by R. Tait McKenzie, who specialised in sculptures of athletes and portrait medals of this kind. Hussey wrote a study of Tait McKenzie in 1929.

The Study

Christopher Hussey wrote and dealt with estate business in this room, which still contains his working library and papers. The room started life as a small drawing room for Edward Hussey III. His daughter-in-law, Rosamond, took her afternoon naps in a deck-chair by the window.

The plasterwork ceiling was designed by Salvin in the Jacobean Revival style of his drawing room at Mamhead in Devon, but features local Kentish hops, modelled freehand. The cream flock wallpaper was supplied by Moxon in 1860. The chimneypiece was originally wood-grained and marbled. It was painted white around 1900. It still has its Salvin fender, which is inscribed 'time tryeth truth as fire gold'.

Books

The glazed bookcase contains Christopher Hussey's extensive collection of early guidebooks. On the shelves to the right of the fireplace are copies of his own work, including a heavily annotated edition of his first important book, *The Picturesque* (1927), together with essential reference sources.

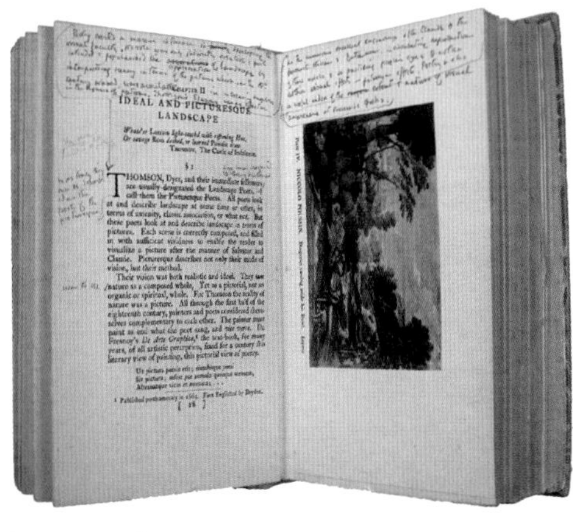

Furniture

The Regency brass-mounted desk was made about 1805, probably by Marsh & Tatham. Christopher Hussey brought it to Scotney.

Pictures

On the wall to the right of the door to the Hall hang Edward Hussey's watercolours of the Old Castle and the New House.

Above Christopher Hussey's own copy of his first important book, *The Picturesque*

Left The Study

Books and more books

'As might be expected in the house of a scholar with such wide tastes as Christopher, the house was full of books. There were books everywhere, and unlike in some houses, they were all books you wanted to read. Books about architecture, about gardening, obscure books of reference, Victorian novels. The books in your bedroom, by your bed, always seemed to have been carefully chosen.'

Peter Coats, 1976

The Library
The Garden Lobby

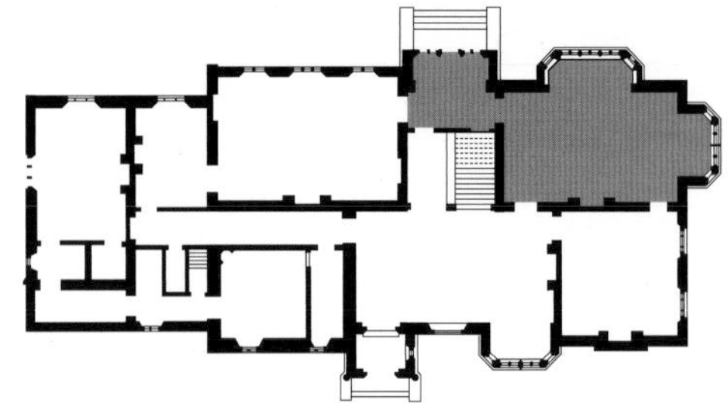

The Library

The Library was intended not just to house the best of the Husseys' books, but also as a comfortable living room. Betty Hussey kept up the tradition, with inviting sofas and a generous drinks trolley. The ornaments betray her love of cats.

The tall bay windows offer superb views south and east over the garden and down to the Old Castle. They were cleverly designed by Salvin to combine the best of old and new – traditional stone mullions above and Victorian plate-glass sliding sashes below for unrestricted enjoyment of the views of the garden and the Old Castle.

The fireplace incorporates old Flemish woodwork with twisted columns. The 'Syrian Damask' wallpaper, designed by the heraldic artist Thomas Willement, was originally crimson and blue on gold, but has faded over the years to a warm brown.

Left The Library

Below Scotney was famous for its hospitality

Opposite left The Husseys' fine library fills the Salvin bookcases

Opposite right Salvin revived the 17th-century fashion for displaying blue-and-white Delftware on brackets

Furniture

Edward Windsor Hussey bought comparatively little furniture, and by the time of his death in 1952 this room was quite sparsely furnished. Betty introduced more seating, covered in a cheerful red printed fabric that was chosen with the help of the interior designer John Fowler.

Books

The bookcases were designed by Salvin to hold Edward Hussey's fine library, which includes numerous volumes on architecture and landscape gardening. Book presses H to J conceal a hidden door, decorated with false spines for such humorous titles as 'Maggots by A. Scollar' and 'Doggerell's Dialogues'.

Christopher Hussey discovers the Picturesque in the Library:

'Through the windows of that room you see in a valley below, a castle, partly ruined on an island in a lake. A balustrade cresting a cliff forms the foreground, a group of Scots firs and limes the side-screens. Beyond, a meadow melts in the woods rising to a high skyline ... it formed the perfect picture ... The very scene before me, so far from being happy co-incidence, must have been planned on picturesque principles.'

The Garden Lobby

This little room below the main stairs provided access to the garden. Old Flemish panelling gives the room a 17th-century character. This is reinforced by the blue-and-white Delftware vases and by the way they are displayed on brackets in the style of the influential late 17th-century interior designer Daniel Marot.

The shallow-vaulted ceiling is in the style of the early 19th-century architect John Soane. The red and green stencilled decoration has been renewed, but faithfully reproduces Salvin's original scheme, which may have been executed by the Crace decorating firm.

Furniture

Salvin made the walnut stools and tables specially for the room in early 17th-century Jacobean style.

The Dining Room
The Small Dining Room

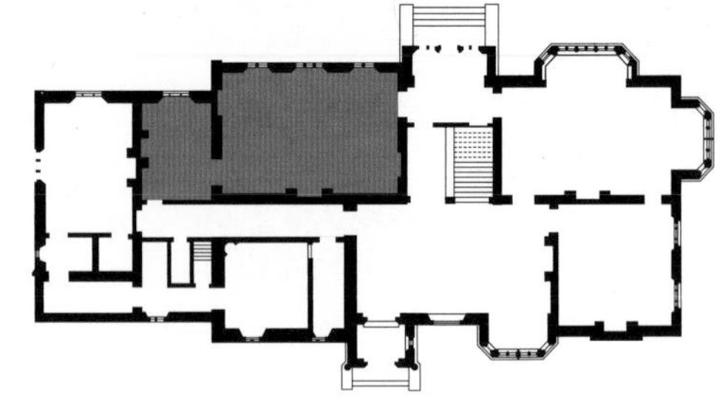

The Dining Room

This is another almost untouched Salvin interior. Of the four doors, only two work – the others are there purely for the sake of symmetry. The plasterwork ceiling is again Jacobean in style.

Furniture

The huge buffet sideboard was made by Salvin for Edward Hussey III, whose portrait hangs over the door.

Pictures

Joachim Beuckelaer (*c.*1534–*c.*1574) specialised in market scenes, in which loving depictions of meat, fruit and vegetables are set in an idealised townscape, with a contrastingly spiritual episode from the life of Christ in the background.

The bizarre vision of dwarfs scrambling among giant melons (over the sideboard) was painted by the north Italian artist Faustino Bocchi (1659–1742). Christopher Hussey bought it about 1920 while he was still a student at Oxford. He became a member of the Magnasco Society, which was founded in 1924 by the writers Osbert and Sacheverell Sitwell to encourage interest in 17th- and 18th-century Italian Baroque painting – then deeply out of fashion.

Opposite top *A Market Scene*; by Joachim Beuckelaer

Opposite below *A Bizarre Landscape with Dwarfs and Melons*; by Faustino Bocchi

Above The Dining Room

Right *An Officer on Horseback*; by Francis Wheatley

The Small Dining Room

Placed between the Kitchen and the Dining Room, this was originally used as a servery, where food would be served up before being brought to table next door. It then became the family's everyday dining room.

Pictures

Over the mantelpiece hangs Francis Wheatley's *Officer on Horseback*. Wheatley specialised in 'portraits in landscapes' of this kind. It may have been painted in Ireland, to which he had fled in 1779 to escape his creditors.

The Service Wing

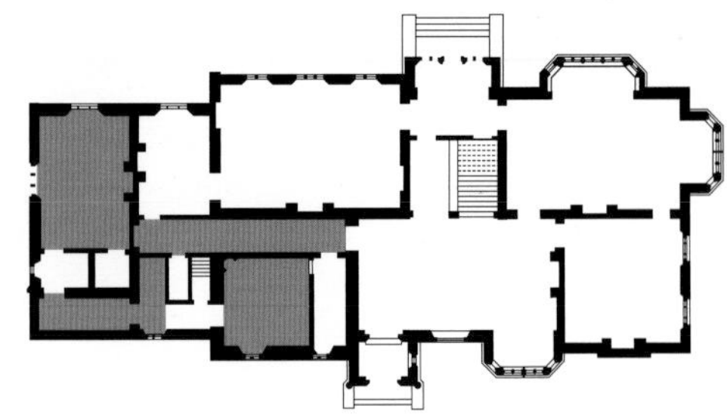

The Kitchen

Betty Hussey was a Cordon Bleu-trained cook and enjoyed cooking and informal dining in the Kitchen, often accompanied by her cat. This room was originally Edward Hussey III's study and was remodelled in the 1950s.

The window behind the sink overlooks the Brewhouse Yard. Edward Hussey could look out from his study and observe the running of the estate. He would also be able to see the activity of the Brewhouse and Dairy located in the buildings opposite. Estate and household business was conducted here. The Servants' Hall and main kitchens were in the adjacent wing, where the servants' bells can be seen today.

Betty upgraded her Kitchen in the 1980s. It was a location for the filming of *Yanks* (1979), starring Richard Gere. She used the fee to pay for the installation of the Aga and kitchen units. Betty was known for her sense of style and eye for colour, which can be seen to good effect in her choice and arrangement of china and kitchen storage jars.

Below left Kitchen shelves displaying brightly coloured china

Below The Kitchen

Opposite centre A plate from the Staffordshire dinner service

Opposite below *Villa Albani, Rome*, 1848; watercolour by Henrietta Windsor-Clive

The Kitchen Lobby and Servants' Corridor

This area was the connection between the main family house and the Service Wing. Part of the set of 19th-century servants' bells can be seen in the corridor, as well as the fire buckets.

The Butler's Pantry

The Butler's Pantry contains an extensive collection of Hussey family china and pottery. This ranges from the best Staffordshire service used by the family on important occasions, to British domestic pottery used latterly for tea parties in the garden.

This has been a butler's pantry since the building of the Salvin house. Prior to the changes made in the 1950s, it is believed there was a hidden upper level in this room which was accessed by a small staircase. The butler would have used this small space as a sleeping cabin.

The room was painted by Sam Beazley for Betty Hussey as part of a series of interiors documenting her life in the house.

The Flower Room

Betty Hussey loved flowers, both real and artificial. This room was created during the 1950s as a space where flowers from the Walled Garden could be arranged. It was also a convenient place for Christopher and Betty to store their coats and boots after a walk across the park.

The Corridor

This narrow passage links the Kitchen with the back stairs and the rest of the house. It is now home to yet more books, many written by friends of the Husseys.

Pictures

Most of the landscape watercolours were painted by Henrietta Windsor-Clive while she was on holiday in Italy in 1848. Shortly afterwards she married Edward Hussey III, builder of the New House, who was also a talented amateur artist.

Ceramics

The shallow vases are Dartmouth pottery made in imitation of Wedgwood black basalt ware.

Conservation in action

Volunteers have been getting involved in helping to preserve the collection. One of the important tasks they have started is checking and cleaning all the books. Each book has to be carefully dusted and checked for signs of damage, insects and mould.

Overleaf Pages from the Husseys' country house albums

SCOTNEY CASTLE,
LAMBERHURST.

Rosamond Hussey

E. W. Hussey

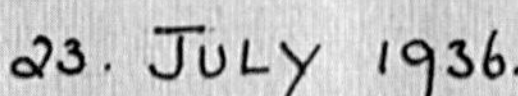

23. JULY 1936.

Henry P. Hussey   Rosamond Hussey

E. W. Hussey   Ralph Toynbee   Bridget Toynbee

SCOTNEY CASTLE,
LAMBERHURST.

4. DECEMBER 1936.

The Staircase Lobby
The Staircase

The Staircase Lobby

In the short passage to the left of the stairs is a very rare ascham – a cupboard used for storing archery equipment. The thirteen bows, two quivers and 50 arrows are believed to have come from Bowman's Lodge, near Dartford, the headquarters of the Royal Kentish Bowmen, which had been founded in 1785 to revive the sport of target archery. Edward Hussey I was an early member.

Pictures

Hanging by the tapestry are small watercolour copies by Mary Anne Herbert, Mrs William Clive Hussey, of portraits at Powis Castle of members of the Clive family.

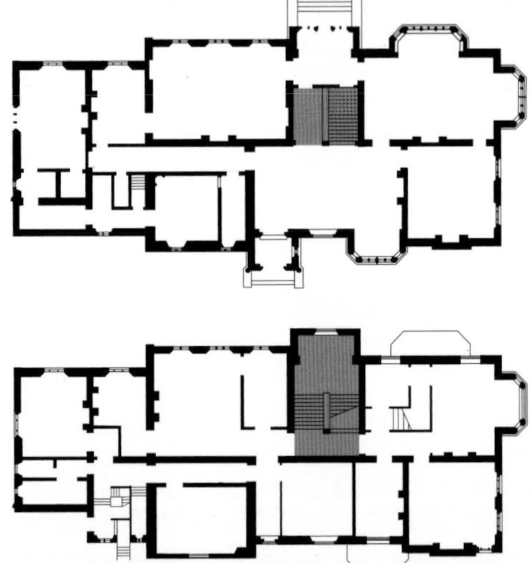

Above *Hallo Largess* (on the Upper Landing) is one of the most famous images of the mid-Victorian working countryside. The artist William Maw Egley witnessed this East Anglian harvest custom in 1860, when visitors gave a present or 'largess' to the harvesters, who acknowledged it with a dance and the cry 'Hallo Largess' (depicted on the right)

The Staircase

Salvin designed the main stairs in a simplified version of the Jacobean style. The pierced newel posts are comparable to those on the contemporary east staircase at Chastleton House in Oxfordshire. The walls were originally painted a stone colour, but were decorated with the present early 19th-century-style damask paper in the 1950s.

Pictures

The large twelve-light window on the half-landing makes this a good place to display pictures.

The portrait of Christopher Hussey was painted in 1964 by his Kentish friend John Ward. He stands in the Library, and the Garden Lobby is visible behind. At his elbow is a copy of his most influential book, on the Picturesque. To the right hangs Simon Elwes's portrait of Betty Hussey as a young woman.

Above Rosamond Anstruther was painted by J.J. Shannon on the terrace at Scotney shortly after her marriage in 1900 to Edward Windsor Hussey. A 1924 portrait of her husband hangs above to the left. Like his more famous contemporary, J.S. Sargent, Shannon was an American artist who made his reputation in Britain painting glamorous portraits of Edwardian high society

Left Sawrey Gilpin, *Gulliver addressing the Houyhnhnms*, 1768. Gilpin tried to raise the low status of horse-painting by finding equine subjects in literature and history. This is taken from Jonathan Swift's satirical novel, *Gulliver's Travels*, and was successful enough to be repeated at least twice

The Dressing Room
The Drawing Room
The Hussey Bedroom
The Bathroom and Wardrobe

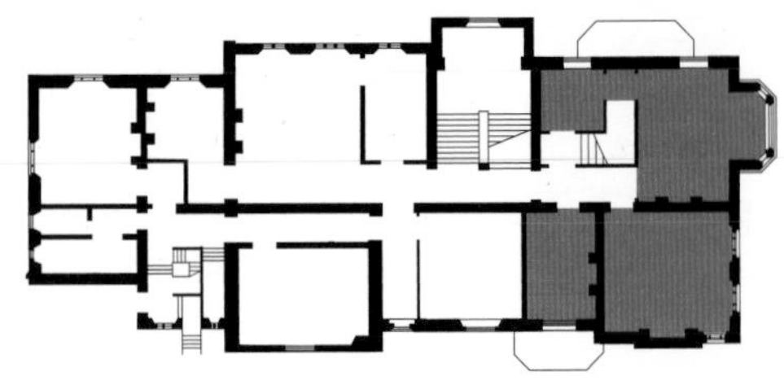

Above The Drawing Room

The Dressing Room

The rooms to the south of the main stairs were originally used as guest bedrooms, but in the 1950s Christopher and Betty Hussey turned them into rooms for themselves.

Christopher Hussey used this modest room as his dressing room, which he decorated with family portraits. Above the fireplace is a view of the High Street in Eton, which was painted by Christopher at the age of fifteen, when he was a pupil there.

The Drawing Room

The Husseys created this informal upstairs sitting room in the 1950s, and furnished it with black lacquer furniture brought from their London home. The cartoonist Osbert Lancaster christened the style 'Vogue Regency'.

Pictures

The views of the Old Castle include colourful watercolours and gouaches by Herbert Alexander (on right-hand wall) and John Piper. Hanging to the left of the entrance door is a chalk drawing of Clive of India's wife, Margaret Maskelyne. Like Betty Hussey, she was a great cat-lover.

Ceramics

The Chinese export porcelain is decorated with the Hussey arms and may have been a wedding present to John and Catherine Hussey, who married in 1796.

The Hussey Bedroom

Immediately above the Library, the bay window of the Husseys' bedroom has an even better view of the Old Castle in the valley below. Mrs Hussey asked that the curtains be left open and the blinds not used, so that visitors might enjoy the view and the light in the room.

Furniture

Scotney has a particularly fine collection of scrap-screens. Many Victorian ladies amused themselves decorating folding screens with 'scraps' – engravings clipped from Christmas cards and other sources. Age and light have damaged the screen, which is now very fragile, demonstrating why it is so important to balance efforts to re-create the atmosphere of a lived-in room with the need to control light levels.

Pictures

These include Regency engravings tracing the tangled course of true love.

The Bathroom and Wardrobe

The Husseys installed the *en suite* bathroom and walk-in wardrobe in the 1950s.

Conservation in action

The black lacquer bureau-cabinet in the Drawing Room was so fragile that a conservator had to face the surface with tissue before it could be moved. It had been damaged by light, central heating, water leaks and heavy use, and had become chipped and worn, with lots of flaking lacquer. It was important not to restore the cabinet to look as new, but to stabilise it, ensuring it matched the 'lived-in' feel of the room.

Above The Hussey Bedroom

Below The set of hair-brushes on Betty Hussey's dressing-table bears her initials

The Red Bathroom
The Red Bedroom
The Green Bedroom

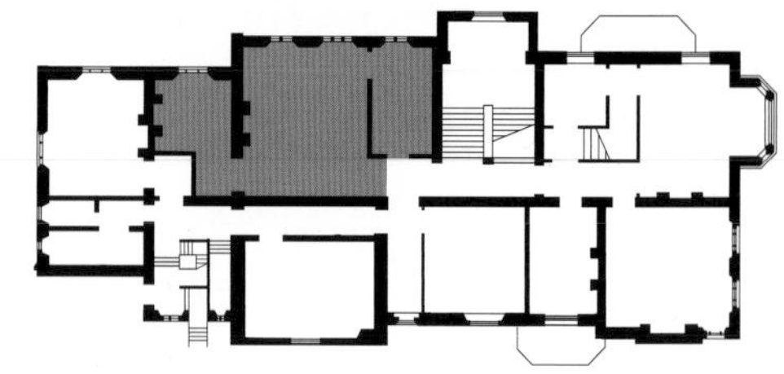

Above The découpage on the scrap-screen in the Red Bedroom

Opposite The half-tester bed and scrap-screen in the Red Bedroom

The Red Bathroom

Originally the dressing room for the Red Bedroom, it was converted into a bathroom in the 1950s. The large cupboard contains bed linen, blankets and quilts. The comic prints over the fireplace are by James Gillray and are thought to have belonged to Edward Hussey III.

The Red Bedroom

In 1954, Christopher and Betty purchased the red poppy wallpaper from their friend John Fowler, the famous country house decorator. In the decoration and arrangement of this bedroom they cleverly united their modern domestic requirements with the older furniture they had inherited, to create the unique red atmosphere.

Furniture

This guest bedroom was originally the master bedroom, the walls decorated by Thomas Willement with 'Valentia Damask' wallpaper. The William IV bed is hung with red chintz, now heavily faded; the day-bed is upholstered to match. On the dressing table are examples of Tunbridge Ware, marquetry pieces made locally for tourists taking the famous spring waters at Tunbridge Wells.

Pictures

Many of the pictures were painted by Henrietta Hussey and her mother Harriet Clive. They include views of Powis Castle, the seat of the Clive family, and Oakley Park, Shropshire, Henrietta's family home. Between the windows is a charming portrait of Gertrude Hussey aged four years, one of the daughters of Edward Hussey III, painted by Albert Ludovici.

The Green Bedroom

This small bedroom with striking floral wallpaper was originally a dressing room connected to the two adjacent bedrooms.

The walls are hung with 19th-century textiles collected by Betty Hussey including samplers and a number of embroidered cats. The unusual felt picture dating from the 1840s depicting a messenger and his donkey is by George Smart, a craftsman based locally in Frant, who produced quirky and humorous fabric pictures for the local tourist industry.

The small lobby beyond houses an extensive collection of 20th-century Penguin Classics and historical novels.

The Bamboo Bedroom
The Friends Bedroom
The Corridor and Salvin Bathroom
The Salvin Bedroom

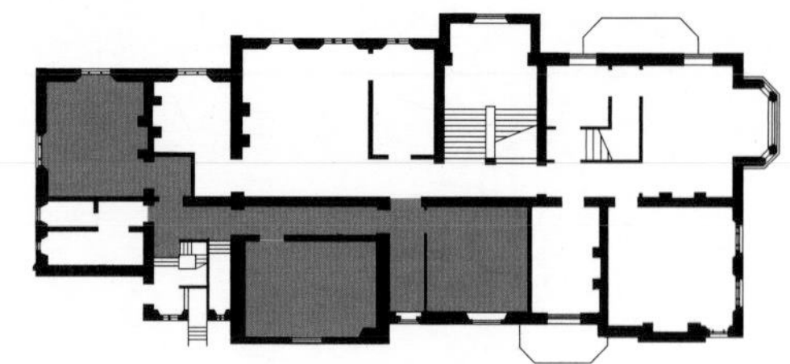

The Bamboo Bedroom

Betty Hussey redecorated this bedroom, taking her inspiration from China. It is the only example of a single decorative scheme that doesn't incorporate 19th-century furniture from the house. The 1951 purchase receipts for the mock-bamboo furniture survive in the collection.

On the Salvin plan this room is called the Boudoir and was probably used by Edward Hussey III's mother Anne. Christopher Hussey believed that the 18th-century fireplace was moved to this room from the Old Castle.

Pictures

Below a portrait of artist Edward Stanley are a series of his watercolours of Spanish and Portuguese scenes, including the famous Alhambra. Below is a detailed panorama of Tunbridge Wells in the 1800s.

Above The Bamboo Bedroom

Opposite The Salvin bed

The Friends Bedroom

The room is largely unaltered from the Salvin design; the only change is the inclusion of a hand basin for guests. The room is filled with pictures by friends of Christopher and Betty Hussey, left behind to thank their hosts for a memorable visit. Some are by famous 20th-century British artists; others are by well-known figures of the day.

Pictures

Over the fireplace are a series of works by John Piper including *Cuckmere Haven* and *Scotney Old Castle*. To the left of the window is a striking portrait of *Miss Josephine* by John Ward. Between the two is a signed landscape of the Greek island of Hydra by cartoonist Sir Osbert Lancaster.

Furnishings

Christopher and Betty furnished this room for the comfort of their guests with a luggage stand at the bottom of the four-poster bed, a radio on the bedside table, and the marquetry bureau at which guests could write letters home. Next door is a small kitchen where the butler could prepare early breakfasts for guests.

The Corridor and Salvin Bathroom

Running along the spine of the main range, this corridor links the main house and what was once the service range. It is furnished with a large mahogany cupboard and many architectural and landscape prints.

In the 1950s the Husseys converted the lavatory into a full bathroom. The 'Ripple' trademark can still be seen on the surviving 19th-century toilet pan.

The Salvin Bedroom

Dominated by a large Salvin-designed four-poster bed, this cluttered guest room evokes the atmosphere of the earlier house. Christopher and Betty brought together the best of what had gone before to preserve these layers of Scotney's history. The 1840s stylised wallpaper clashes dramatically with the lighter floral chintz hangings from 1907.

The room is furnished with many personal treasures and keepsakes directly connected to three generations of the Hussey family. These include Italian plaster cameos thought to have been acquired by Edward Hussey III on his tour of Europe and an oak fire-screen bearing the initials of his wife Henrietta. A portrait of Rosamund Hussey as a child hangs over the fireplace, a copy of the original that was once here. In front of the window is a seven-part ivory dressing-table set bearing the monogram MKS that belonged to Betty's mother, Maud Kerr-Smiley. To the left of this is a needlepoint picture of 6 Swan Walk completed by Betty in 1935, the year before her marriage to Christopher.

The Bastion View
The Quarry Garden

The Bastion View

The Bastion, a semi-circular balustrade, gives the classic view of the garden stretching down to the Old Castle at the bottom of the valley. The garden ends at the river and the park rises beyond to woods of beech and oak.

The same trees covered the parkland that existed here before Edward Hussey III returned in 1835 with the intention of creating a new house and garden. His approach was influenced by contemporary writings on the Picturesque, such as Uvedale Price's *Essays on the Picturesque* and Richard Payne Knight's *Inquiry on Taste*. He sought advice from the artist and landscape gardener William Sawrey Gilpin, but also used his own talents as a watercolourist, and the 'pleasure garden' would ultimately stem from Edward's personal Picturesque vision. The men of the family would use the garden for outdoor pursuits such as shooting rabbits, while the women and children would practise the more genteel outdoor pursuit of horticulture in the Walled Garden, built in 1840.

Edward Windsor Hussey made gradual acquisitions that enriched the colour and texture of the garden, but allowed it to mature following his father's design. Christopher and Betty Hussey also wished to restore and enrich the garden according to its founding principles. They planted many bulbs to lengthen the season of interest, opened up more views of the Old Castle, added to the number of rare and interesting plants, increased the areas of beds and added more flowering plants, especially roses.

Before the storm of October 1987, the tall and vertical lines of cedars of Lebanon, Scots pines and Lawson cypresses provided a 'frame' for the view from the Bastion. Replacements have been planted to restore it without filling and obscuring the present, more open view. Climbing, floribunda and shrub roses surround the Venetian font, which was placed opposite the lion's mouth fountain by Edward Windsor Hussey in 1898. The Top Walk is planted with flowering trees and shrubs, including magnolias, tulip trees and an impressive *Paulownia tomentosa*, and offers views across to the hilltop church at Goudhurst.

The Quarry Garden

When stone for the New House was removed and the quarry created, the fossilised remains of a 'ripple bed' were uncovered, dating from the Mesozoic geological era, when Scotney was on the shore of a great sea that stretched between here and Belgium. As the ocean tide receded, it left ripples on the sand, which became stone over millions of years. Footprints left in the sand were also revealed and identified as belonging to the herbivore Iguanodon. A popular story has early palaeontologist Gideon Mantell discovering the first Iguanodon teeth in 1822 about 30 miles away in Cuckfield, West Sussex.

Above The steps up to the Quarry Garden

Opposite Azaleas and rhododendrons in the Quarry Garden

At the turn of the Millennium the quarry suffered a serious rock fall after being weakened by the roots of the trees that grew on the rim above it. Following a wet winter and severe frost, between 20 and 30 tons of rock collapsed, exposing what can be seen today. After the rubble had been cleared away, terraces were created to help with the replanting. The shade and moistness of the quarry make it an ideal home for many types of fern, along with large specimens of April-flowering *Magnolia stellata* and fragrant Ghent azaleas of yellow, cream and orange. High summer brings rhododendrons and willow gentians of white and blue.

Massed clumps of *Ponticum* rhododendrons, favoured by the Picturesque designers, bloom in shades of mauve, purple, rose and white in May. June showcases the famous calico pink and white bell-like flowers of *Kalmia latifolia*, and late summer brings intense blue tones of hydrangeas. Autumn follows with the rich reds and golds of *Nyssa sylvatica*, liquidambars and Japanese maples.

Current developments

The garden at Scotney is constantly evolving, with several areas being reinstated to the original plans of around 1877.

One of the larger projects that we are currently undertaking is the restoration of the Walled Garden, which involves returning this area to a working vegetable garden. We have recently discovered plans dating from 1840, which was when the Walled Garden was completed. These show not only the layout of the vegetable beds, but also the varieties of fruit trees that were trained along the walls. We plan to reinstate these features and source as many of the old varieties of fruit, vegetables and fruit trees as possible, and then replant the Walled Garden to its original design.

We have also discovered a sunken way which lies along the southern side of the terrace, and we believe this to be one of the original Picturesque entrances into the garden. As this is a new discovery, we need to undertake further archaeological surveys of this area to find out more about what it would have looked like. With careful restoration work, we will reinstate this sunken pathway as a route through the garden.

The 1877 plan and a description in the archives reveal that the garden originally had flowing views out into the park and over the landscape towards Goudhurst and the wider estate. Unfortunately, over the years *Rhododendron ponticum* has obscured these views and has screened the garden from the surrounding landscape. Our long-term policy is to reduce and remove the overgrown shrubs and re-establish the original form of this Picturesque garden.

‘The quarry long neglected, and o’ergrown
With thorns, that hang o’er mould’ring beds of stone,
May oft the place of nat’ral rocks supply,
And frame the verdant picture to the eye.’

Richard Payne Knight (1794)

The Old Castle

'The lily-moat reflecting the grey and rust-coloured mansion, sky, and trees, against a steep wilderness of quarry and towers today makes an exquisite picture. If ever ruin-making has justified itself, this has.'

Rose Macaulay, *Pleasures of Ruins* (1953)

The Lime Tree Walk leads down to the Old Castle. When Edward Hussey purchased Scotney in 1778, 'the mansion house' was described as being:

> lately substantially repaired and surrounded by a large Moat of running water, well stocked with Fish; in the Moat an Island, and a Chinese Bridge over a small River; the ground floor consists of Front and Back kitchens etc., Housekeeper's room, a Parlour; on the first Floor, 2 Parlours, a large dining room, a Breakfast and 2 Dressing-rooms, 5 Bedchambers, a Study and Library; on the second Floor, 8 rooms; Kitchen and Pleasure gardens within the moat, planted with plenty of Fruit trees and Flowers; without the Gates a Garden, Shrubbery, Warren, Orchard, coach-house, Brew-house, Stabling for 8 horses and other offices; a cold Bath with an excellent Mineral Well of the same quality as that at Tunbridge Wells.

Rejecting the option of demolishing the Old Castle, Edward Hussey III decided to transform it into a romantic ruin, the centrepiece of the new garden. Masonry, vegetation and water would all be used to compose a picture in the same way that, as a watercolourist, he used pigments. The three-storeyed 17th-century range was demolished, allowing the older and more striking features of the Ashburnham Tower (built from Hastings bed sandstone) and south wing to dominate. The south wing continued to be occupied, first by the Head Gardener George Wells and then by the Estate Bailiff until 1905. The evidence of their habitation, such as a smoking chimney, added a final touch to the Picturesque view. Christopher and Betty Hussey used it to store and display items they felt were superfluous in their modernising of the New House such as hunting trophies.

American garden designer Lanning Roper became friends with Christopher and Betty Hussey in 1952 and made regular visits. He began to remake the herb garden in 1970 around the carved Venetian well-head, which had been placed there by Christopher Hussey's aunt. Along with herbs, such as rosemary, are scented geraniums and heliotropes. Around the moat are water-loving plants, including yellow irises in spring, royal ferns that turn dark brown in autumn, and rodgersia and king-cups. The ruined east range displays honeysuckle in winter and early spring, while summer brings out displays of climbing roses, vines, *Celastrus orbiculatus* and white Chinese wisteria. Late summer sees the mulberry tree bearing fruit.

Opposite The ruins of the Old Castle

Left A view through an Old Castle window in spring

Below The Venetian well-head

The Moat

The moat was formed when the small River Bewl was dammed. In 1863 it was joined with the stewponds that surrounded the isthmus where there now stands the Henry Moore sculpture. The stewponds had been created in the Middle Ages to serve as a source of fish, which the Catholic Darell family required for their Friday meals.

The Bridge Walk leads on to the Chinese bridge that spans the moat. Already here when the Husseys bought the house, the present one is a wooden replacement for the rustic original. In the foreground to the left is the gabled wooden boathouse, and beyond is the Ashburnham Tower reflected in the moat. On the opposite side can be seen the bronze *Three Piece Reclining Figure – Draped,* by Henry Moore. Originally planted with rhododendrons, the isthmus was cleared in 1977 to make way for the sculpture, given by Moore in memory of his friend Christopher Hussey. A path runs between the south side of the Moat and the River Bewl, offering another famous view of the Old Castle in the foreground and a gabled corner of the New House in the background behind the Quarry.

Opposite A boating party on the moat

Below The *Three Piece Reclining Figure,* by Henry Moore, 1977

Right The boathouse

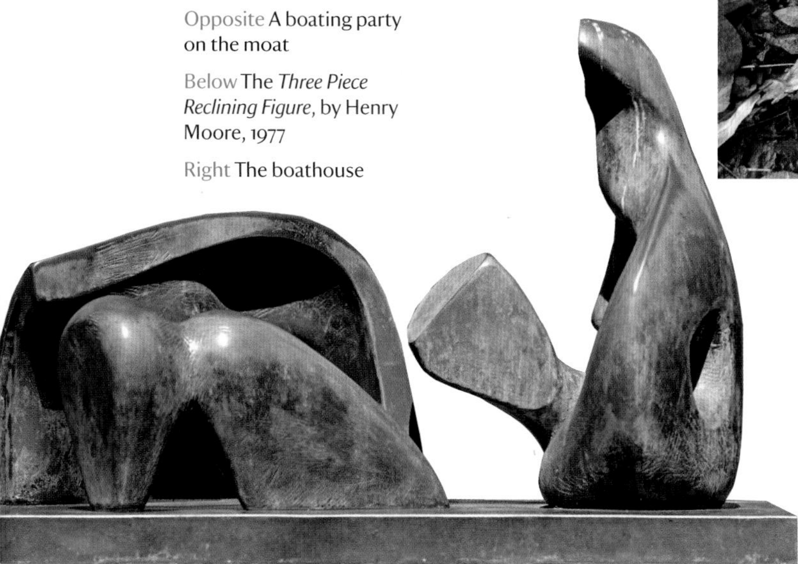

Standing on the north-east corner of the moat is the tent-shaped ice-house, built in 1839 and thatched with heather. The 13ft pit was lined with straw, and a cross framework of joists filled in with hop poles, or binders, allowed for drainage. Ice was taken from the moat in winter and placed here for storage. In the days before modern refrigeration it provided the Husseys with a convenient supply of ice for use in the kitchen during the summer.

The Estate

The diverse Scotney estate is made up of farmland, woodland and Grade I listed parkland, much of which is designated as a Site of Special Scientific Interest (SSSI). Over the years, the estate has been put to a wide range of uses: areas have been heathland, oak and hornbeam coppice, woodland pasture and hop gardens. In recent times, the estate has concentrated on its herd of Sussex cattle, hops and woodland.

Little Scotney Farm has always had a herd of Sussex cattle, and during the time of Christopher Hussey these were regular prize-winners at agricultural shows. We have reinstated the herd, which can be seen grazing in the parkland.

Scotney Castle is the only National Trust-owned working hop farm, and still uses the original round oast-houses to dry the hops. These hops go to produce Scotney Ale, Scotney Bitter and Viceroy Beers. At the height of the hop industry in 1878, this part of Kent was where world hop prices were set. Since then, the British hop industry has declined by 94 per cent.

The woodlands are predominantly made up of Sweet Chestnut coppice, which was planted for the hop industry, and since its decline has been used in part for fencing materials. Now the woodlands are being managed for sustainable fuel for the Scotney biomass boiler, as well as still supplying fence poles. This means that many of the buildings at Scotney are now heated by woodchip provided by the estate.

Looking out on the estate and while walking through it, you may encounter many different types of wildlife. We are lucky enough to have fallow and roe deer, dormice, badgers and great crested newts. Some of the rarer species are the brilliant emerald dragonfly and green-winged orchid. There is always something to see; you may just have to look for it!

All of the estate can be explored easily by following way-marked routes.

Above Green-winged orchid

Below left Female brilliant emerald dragonfly

Below right Dormouse hibernating

Opposite The woodland at dawn